I0004538

HTML Awesomeness Book

Learn to write HTML the awesome way

Gilad E. Tsur Mayer

Copyright © 2016 by Gilad E. Tsur Mayer

Stop Everything! I Have a Present For You!

Omg omg omg!! Aren't you excited?! I *love* presents!

This book will get you to know HTML, but personally I prefer videos over books - it's easier if someone does all the work of reading for you, right? You can watch a bunch of videos and in no time you will be an expert.

So, I took this book, and blended it all into a bite-sized video course, so if you will watch it, you will know every basic building block of HTML in no time! Neat, huh?

And because you have purchased *this* book, I will give you 50% off this video course. Awesome, right?

Grab the videos here: http://basichtml.gilad.me/discount50/

Table of Contents

Introduction

Hey Guys!

Welcome to the HTML Awesomeness Book, where you will learn to write the basics of HTML, the awesome way.

My name is Gilad, and I will lead you through this amazing book!

I began my career as a web developer, but soon transitioned to entrepreneurship, where I founded my very own startup company.

Currently, I work at the company I've founded from scratch, and also I do what I love the most: teaching you guys!

I designed this book for anyone seeking to learn basic HTML and begin a career as a rockstar web developer, as well as anybody who just loves to expand their knowledge.

By the end of the book, you will have a rock solid knowledge of all HTML building blocks such as:

- HTML Titles
- HTML Links
- HTML images
- HTML Forms
- And many many more..

I will teach you the latest version of HTML5 by the standards of the W3C Association. These standards are used by all the major companies in the world.

The ideal student for this book is anybody who wants to expand their knowledge of HTML or get a leg up in the web developer world.

There are no prerequisites necessary to enroll but I do request that you come open-minded to my silly jokes!

You are free to take a look at the book description, and I look forward to meeting you inside.

Why Learn HTML Anyway ?

You might ask yourself, why should I learn HTML anyway, right?

Well, if you do, don't be shy, it's a valid question. And I will try to address it in this topic.

Nowadays, everything is on the Internet, and in this magical place, the only language is HTML!

You may go some website on your mobile phone: that's written in HTML!

You may order some tickets to the concert that you always wanted to see... The ticket website was written in HTML!

Heck! Nowadays, even mobile games have HTML in them!

HTML may be the only language that hasn't gone extinct since the dawn of the internet in the early 90's.

What is HTML?

So now you know why you should learn HTML, let's dig a lil' bit deeper and understand what HTML is.

The abbreviation HTML is actually used because of a "marketing decision", you know, "HyperText Markup Language" is not very catchy to some people... go figure, huh?

Let's break it down:

- *HyperText* is the method by which you move around on the web, you click on one link, and then in some sort of magic you go to another page, and so on, and so forth..
- *Markup* is for HTML **Tags**. Tags are what the language of HTML is made of. (Don't worry, I'll explain to you later in this book what a Tag is.)
- *Language*, well... HTML is indeed a language that our beloved browsers understand.

Where are you now? (BONUS! Woohoo!)

I believe that if you want to *REALLY* understand something, you have to get what I call "the big picture..."

HTML is a powerful language that you may know, but there is a big picture for it, if you want to be a web developer!

To be frank, you don't *HAVE* to understand it. So if you want to skip to the next topic, it's OK! (I'll be disappointed though, I've made lots of effort to write this down!)

But, I do encourage you broaden your knowledge a bit, and see what you can learn next.

HTML and CSS:

So, *HTML* is what you see when you first open a webpage!

But *HTML* has a close "friend" called "*CSS.*"

They come together, like peas and carrots (Thanks, Forrest Gump!) and the reason for this is because *HTML* in charge of the *structure* of the page, and *CSS* is in charge of the *design* of it. For example, you might have a great *HTML* header with your name on it, and the *CSS* to paint it blue.

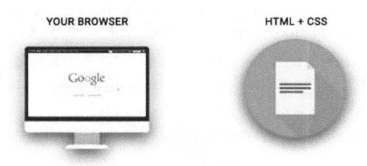

YOUR BROWSER   HTML + CSS

Server Side or Javascript:

Next up, you have the logic of the webpage, and it's divided into two parts: *Javascript*, and *Server Side* (which can vary from website to website).

Let me set up a "real world" situation so you can understand it better. Let's say you have a great website. You set up its structure, and then you designed it with *CSS*, and then in the bottom of the page, you have big gray "Submit" button. And you want your users to press the submit button, and then get ... the current time. I don't know why you would do this, but let's say you do!

You have to somehow set a simple logic to your webpage to grab the current time from somewhere, and then send it back to your *HTML* and *CSS* to present it, right?

That's why you have that logic!

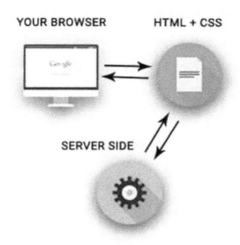

YOUR BROWSER   **HTML + CSS**

SERVER SIDE

Databases:

So you have your web page structured and designed by your HTML and CSS, you have your logic with *Javascript* or *Server Side*, and now you want to save your user's username, and then welcome them every time they click on your website, with "Howdy, johnny4589!". How are you gonna do that?

Well, when your user enters your page with their username and password, you send the *server side* the details that the user typed inside of your *HTML* and then the *Server Side* requests the details stored in the *Database* of this specific username, then it sends the name back into this pipeline, until it gets back to the *HTML*, and *HTML* presents it (and the *CSS* makes it look pretty)!

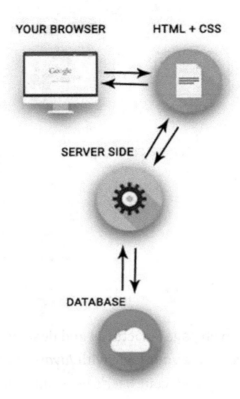

YOUR BROWSER   HTML + CSS

SERVER SIDE

DATABASE

Do I need a special program to use HTML?

So I bet so far you are sold about learning *HTML*, and join the gang of the Web Development world.

But you are probably asking, "what software do I need before I can start *HTML*ing?" And the answer is: nothing!

Almost all computers come with some basic tools necessary to start to write *HTML*. if you have a PC using Windows, you can use *Notepad*. And if you have Mac, you can use *TextEdit*.

Personally, I like to use Notepad++. It's powerful free software for PCs.

(You can download it for free here: https://notepad-plus-plus.org/download/)

I will use Notepad++ on every example shown in this book. But you can use whatever software you like.

To open your code with your browser, just right click on your .txt file, and select "open with..". Then select your favorite browser.

HTML Tags (self closing) and Elements

OMG! OMG! OMG! OMG!!!....I'm sooo excited!

You are all set with your shiny Notepad++, you know everything you need to know about how it all connects to other components of web development, AND.... you are ready to go with tons of enthusiasm.

What more can an instructor ask for?!

Tags & Elements

Let's dive into writing HTML code!

Remember the "M" on HTML? We talked about it, and agree it represent the word Markup, which is Tags... And here we are, learning about Tags! So what are Tags?

Tags are things between open angle brackets "<" and closing angle brackets ">".

I'm sure you've seen such code in movies and stuff, and if you didn't (and even if you did!), you are more than welcome to right click on *every* website, and click on *"View Source"* option.

Tags are everywhere on HTML, and they are basically the most important building block of HTML. which every word inside of these weird angle brackets, makes a different meaning of tag.

Most of the tags (and we will soon see why it's most of them, and not all of them) have closing tags. For example :

```
<em> </em>
```

You can think of it, as a way that we are trying to say to the browser, "OK, Browser! Now we want to start doing something…" and "All right Browser! You can now stop doing what I told you to do!"

Note that the difference between the opening tag to the closing tag is that little forward slash.

Together, the opening tag and the closing tag make up a perfect couple called an "HTML element."

Let's try our very first HTML element! Write inside of your text editor:

```
I like bananas,<em> but only when it
rains.</em>
```

And if you will refresh your page, you will see that indeed we have regular text for the part that says "I like bananas," but when it says "but only when it rains.", the HTML rendered it differently, with a lil' bit of emphatic flair!

All that, thanks to our beloved HTML elements!

I like bananas, *but only when it rains.*

Self Closing Elements

We've seen that elements have an opening tag, a closing tag, and between them is the content we are manipulating (not evilly!).

But some elements do not carry any content inside of them!

Let's have an example!

```
My squirrel <hr/> has 3 eyes!
```

If we will render the our browser, we will be witness to a horizontal line, thanks to the self-closing element of the *hr* tag. Note that the the element has no closing tag, only one tag. And instead of a forward slash before the *hr*, we have it after the *hr*.

We have a few self closing elements in HTML, and we will bump some of them in this book as well! Yay!

Nested Elements

In some cases, you will want to manipulate your HTML with the power of more than one element. If that's the case, you can use the nested element technique.

Let me show you an example :

```
I had to
<b>
        drive on my
```

```
        <em>hamster-mobile.</em>
</b>
I got into an accident with a donkey.
```

Let's refresh the page and see what we've got here:

First we typed "I had to" in regular fashion, and then we started to use the *b* tag. Which made our text look bold from now on, and until we bumped the closing tag of the *b* element.

And indeed we see on our page, that the "drive on my" is bolded text. But then we have the em element, inside of the b element, which cause the text to be bolded AND emphasized!

My oh my!

That's a powerful technique! Glad we covered it!

Attributes

Sometimes you will want to provide additional information to your HTML element.

You can achieve it with an HTML attribute.

For example:

```
<p title="not really! :D" >
        Robot flirting with my car
</p>
```

In this example, clearly my Robot is flirting with my car. But if you will look closely, and hover your mouse over the text in the web page, you will see a tooltip saying "not really!" with a strange looking smiley face! This is because we added a "title" attribute which lets the browser act as a tooltip.

Attributes have criteria:

- • ⍰ They will come only on the opening tag

- • ⍰ You have a key and a value. In this example, the key is "title" and the value is "not really" with a weird smiley face in addition. The equals sign separates the key from the value.

- • ⍰ And last, you can add as many attributes as you want! Yay!

ID Attribute

When I was a child, I had a friend that had an identical twin brother. Sometimes, I was very confused and thought my friend was his brother, and vice versa!

So I made up a system to remember him by! My friend had a lil' mole right over his left eyebrow.

Just like my fictitious genetically-weird friend, your elements could be practically identical to your other elements.

Which could cause confusion if you try to add a bit of design for it later in *CSS* or make up some logic with *Javascript.*

Here is an example of what I mean:

```
<p id="salty_fox1" > paragraph one </p>
<p id="salty_fox2" > paragraph two </p>
```

In this example we have two lines of text. On the surface, it seems like you cannot tell the difference between them (except that one says "paragraph one" and the other "paragraph two." But each line has a different id. This is very important. And you will come across this problem later in your career, when you combine your HTML with other snippets of code such as *CSS* or *Javascript,* And we will explore it further in the intermediate book.

By the way, you can grab a 50% coupon for it right here:

http://basichtml.gilad.me/discount50/

How to set up your page

Alright, so far we've learned about HTML, HTML tags, HTML elements, and even Attributes!

But we didn't talk about how it all comes together.

Type this in your text editor:

```
<!DOCTYPE html>
<html>
        <head>
        </head>
        <body>
        </body>
</html>
```

What you see now, in its simplest form, is the example of HTML document.

You can save it, and use it whenever you want to start writing HTML.

Let's get through every element, and see what we have here :

• ⬚ The *!DOCTYPE* declaration, defines what version of HTML we are using. All you need to know is that this tag is telling the browser the version of HTML you want to use. Just stick this in, and that's it. Oh, and one more thing: note that it's not really an element, it's a tag, without a closing tag. That's the only tag you will see acting weirdly that way.

• ⬚ Immediately after the *doctype declaration*, we have the the root of all of the HTML elements (with the best HTML tag name of them all): the **html** element. The html element summons all the other elements nested inside it.

• ⬚ The **head** element is where your HTML stores all of its "settings." This is where you can find all of the metadata, all of the titles, links, scripts, and styles.

• ⬚ The almighty **body** element is where the rest of your code will be. This is where you will most often write. You two will be the best friends ever! You will write inside of this element, all the time!

HTML Title

I never seen another website or a webpage without a decent title decorating the browser tab.

If you would like to have your own webpage title, type in your text editor the following code:

```
<!DOCTYPE html>
<html>
        <head>
            <title>Welcome to the stinky cottage
                    cheese website!</title>
        </head>
        <body>
        </body>
</html>
```

Save your document, and refresh your page and see what changed in your browser.

You can enjoy a brand new title in your browser tab, named "Welcome to the stinky cottage cheese website!" And what a welcome that would be! Imagine that...

Just like we said earlier about elements, we have the opening element `<title>` then the content, our text welcoming us to our stinky cottage cheese website, and then in the end the `</title>` closing tag.

Note that just like we said before, the *head* element holds all of the "settings" so to speak of our webpage. So a tab title is indeed a setting. So we placed it in the head element.

Paragraph tag

All right! Let's add some text to our website, shall we?

Type that in your text editor:

```
<!DOCTYPE html>
<html>
        <head>
                <title>Welcome to the stinky
cottage cheese website!</title>
        </head>

        <body>
                My piano swallowed my teeth.

                I wonder why it needs them.
</body>

</html>
```

Save it, refresh your page, and see what we have done.

Oh, snap! Somehow my browser interpreted my piano text all wrong!

I wanted my text to be two lines separated from each other, and it (quite rudely, I must say!) presented it as huge one line.

What gives? Well, HTML ignores all new lines, spaces, and stuff like that..

For those kind of tasks, we have our *paragraph* tag.

The paragraph tag represented by the letter p, and allow us to differentiate one paragraph from another.

Add this to your code :

```
<p>My piano swallowed my teeth.</p>
<p>I wonder why it needs them.</p>
```

Now save it and refresh your page, and voila! We have two separate lines!

HTML Break Line & HTML Horizontal Line

Now we want to make our two lines have more space between them.

```
<p>My piano swallowed my teeth.</p>
<br/>
<p>I wonder why it needs them. </p>
```

Save it and refresh the page.

Wow, that was easy!

Due to the `<br/>` tag we can create a new line, push more our paragraph from each other, and even break our line of text in the middle of the sentence! Look:

```
<p>My piano swallowed <br/> my teeth.</p>
<br/>
<p>I wonder why it needs them. </p>
```

Did you see that?! Oh man... almost magical!

By the way, you can see that our BR tag is a self closing tag, because it does not hold any content, just like we learned in the previous lesson!

HTML Heading

Now that we have a title tab, we also want our current page will be decorated with a title heading!

To do this sort of task you will need to type this in your text editor :

```
<h1> The Broccoli Dilemma </h1>
```

Save your file, refresh your page, and let's see what we have got here:

Oh wow! A huge beautiful suspicious title says we have a dilemma with our broccoli. Why a dilemma you may ask? I ask that too.

Anyway, we have more heading tags: *h2, h3, h4, h5* and *h6*.

All of those are sub-headings, with different sizes. See for yourself!

HTML List

Every year I have new things I want to do for the upcoming year.

I grab a pen and paper and try to imagine what I can do this year that will be great and exciting!

Well, this year we are going to write down my list in HTML!

Type this in your text editor :

```
<ul>
     <li> Hire two private investigators.
          Get them to follow each other.</li>
     <li> Change name to Simon. Speak in third
person.</li>
     <li> Stop making lists.</li>
</ul>
```

Alright! So we have our our list, note that we have nested elements here.. we have got the ul tag, which means that we want our list to be "Unordered List". And inside, we have li tag, which means "List Item".

Just like the *Unordered List*, we have also *Ordered List*.

Let's order our list from the most exciting thing to the least exciting thing to do next year.

```
<ol>
     <li> Stop making lists.</li>
```

```
    <li> Change name to Simon. Speak in third
person.</li>
    <li> Hire two private investigators.
    Get them to follow each other.</li>
</ol>
```

All right! So we have in the first place, hands down, the best thing to do next year:

"Stop making lists!" Wow, I can't wait to make that a reality!

Then we have the second round, "Change my name to Simon. Speak in third person," that would be awesome!

And then, last but not least! "Hire two private investigators, get them to follow each other." Imagine that, eh ?

HTML Images

There is no cool website that lacks images! In this lesson we will try to place a great image into our website.

Take a photo of yourself and place the image file in your website folder with the name "me.jpg". Then, in your text editor, type:

```
<img src="me.jpg" alt="my picture" />
```

Now save your file and refresh.

And look at that.. Who is this great-looking web developer?! A great photo!

Let's dig down and see what we have right here in the code.

First things first, we have the img tag. As you can imagine, img is a shorthand for image. No big deal.

Then, we have two attributes inside of this tag. We can also see that our img element is a self closing element, which kinda make sense, because it's not holding any information..

The src attribute is a source. Which means that this is where the image file is located.

And the alt, means alternative text. At times the image might not load for whatever reason, and the browser will show your alt text instead.

HTML Comments

In the near future you might work as a web developer on a project. And in this project you will work with more developers.

In that case, communication is key.

Because of that, we have comments inside our HTML.

Here's an example :

```
<!-- delete before publish -->
<p> Can't wait to hand my frog a gold medal</p>
```

As you can see I have a paragraph that says that I cannot wait to hand my frog a gold medal. Which is a very normal thing to do.

But right above this paragraph, I have a comment, which clearly says to delete the paragraph before publishing the web page. Now, I can write anything I want in this comment, its sole purpose is for me, or for my colleagues to see, and act accordingly. Furthermore, it won't be visible on my webpage in any shape or form.

HTML Links

Oh my, oh my... this is VERY exciting.. This is all very exciting , we are heading into one of the very great things about the internet: links!

You know that feeling that you are going to wikipedia and then clicking around, and then five minutes later you find yourself reading about hamsters in Namibia?! Right? Well, this is the power of links!

And we will learn it here in this lesson!

So, open your text editors, and type this:

```
<a href="http://www.gilad.me">Udemy Link</a>
```

Now save your file and refresh your documents and behold!

A link! Oh wow!

Now let's examine this link , shall we ?

We have the a element, which is a link element.

Than we have an attribute named href, and the content that we typed there.

The href attribute holds my link path - the address of the website that you will see if you will click the link.

And the content will be what you will see on the website usually in a blue, underlined text.

Forms

Do you know all of these daunting websites that require you to place your your username, first name, and stuff like that?

Well, today we will be daunting as well, and we will be build a form like that!

Type this in your text editor :

```
<form>
        Full Name:  <br/>
        <input type="text" placeholder="Full
        Name" />
        <br/>
        What is my Favorite Color?
        <select>
                <option>Choose One..</option>
                <option>Black</option>
                <option>Blue</option>
                <option>Orange</option>
                <option>I'm color blind!</option>
        </select>
        <br/>
        Will you give my soul to me?  <br/>
        <input type="checkbox"
        checked="checked"/>
        <br/>
```

```
        <input type="submit" value="Do it!" />
</form>
```

Save it, refresh it, and let's examine what's going on!

On our root element we have our form tag.

Inside of the form tag, we have several Input tags, these are self closing elements.

The first one is input tag typed "text", which is a tag that allows us to have a textbox. It also has the placeholder attribute. That will make a cool placeholder effect (by the way, this works only on newer browsers, so don't freak out if nothing shows up).

The other input tag, is the checkbox. It has a checked attribute, that makes you have the checkbox checked in advanced.

We also have a nested HTML element called select element.

The select element is a special element that tells the browser to render a multi-select list (or a drop-down list). Nested inside of this element is the the option tag. Each option tag specifies the... options in the dropdown list (surprise-surprise, eh?)

And the last input tag, is the input tag type submit, which is a submit button to send everything into the server side, if we had any.

Now what ?

Congratulations!

You accomplished this book, you heard lots of bad jokes in this book, and I'm very proud of you!

You might ask yourself:

Now, that I've accomplished my first HTML book, what should I do now? How can I improve my web developing skills? Well, my young padawan, now it's time to combine your HTML skills with some CSS.

I do have a CSS book just for you, and because you purchased this book (or in compensation for my bad jokes), I will give you 50% off all of my books in Udemy.

Just email me at: http://basichtml.gilad.me/discount50/ and ask for the discount!